MW01595992

STORY OF THESE WALLS

written by
Jason David

co-written with
Alyson Ramos & Ryan Hicks

edited by
Lynda Wright & Ryan Hicks

photo by
Marissa Juarez

graphic design by
Jason David

published by
Jason David Music

Stay connected on social media
@JasonDavidMusic

Find original music, inspiring talks & booking inquiries
at **JasonDavidMusic.com**

Dedicated to my hero,
Alyson

Published by JASON DAVID MUSIC in 2020

PART ONE:

Surviving Seagulls

I've been bitten by a seagull.

I've been attacked by a puppy.

I've been stung by a bee, sprayed by a skunk, chased by a beaver, ambushed by a possum, sabotaged by a rabbit, kicked by a sheep, tackled by a full grown Rottweiler and surrounded by three sharks off the coast of La Jolla.

I'm a survivor.

On a road trip with friends I tried to feed a flock of selfish birds at a rest stop near Camp Pendleton. One eager seagull came in for a nibble, and must have had poor depth perception, because he missed the bread and bit my finger instead. Poor eyesight... they don't call them "see" gulls.

While hiking I came across a puppy. He was lost. I was lonely. I reached for his collar. He reached for my hand... with his teeth!

3

In junior high, while feeling like a daredevil, I ran as fast as I could near a beehive to see what would happen. Turns out... I'm an idiot.

As a wedding gift my brother-in-law bought me a bunny. Weeks later I lost my new floppy-eared baby black bunny in the backyard. When I thought I had spotted him, I rushed in to the rescue. Did you know dark furry butts all look the same? I found that out when my so called baby bunny turned out to be an angry skunk with B.O. My wife and I quickly ran inside the house for protection. We grabbed the nearest weapons we could find from the kitchen. Avocados. We ran back outside and began chucking our weaponized groceries in the general direction of the smelly imposter. The following morning we checked the backyard, only to discover half-eaten avocados. I guess skunks eat healthy produce from Trader Joe's just like us. We often have so much in common with our enemies.

My favorite animal is a river otter. A cute furry brown little guy who swims, walks, and at all times appears adorable. I'd met a few of them at Sea World on my fourteenth birthday. It was love at first sight. My life long goal became finding an endangered river otter in the wild. And so it was, just two years later, I found myself at Lake Navajo, while boating with my grandparents. It was lunch time. My grandad pulled into a secret cove. My grandma prepared spaghetti and meatballs. I patrolled the perimeter, on the lookout for strange and wonderful creatures. That's when I saw him! In the wild and in the flesh, I couldn't believe my eyes, but there he was, swimming! I quickly grabbed my grandma's yellow floaty and swam out to meet him. My palms were sweaty. Knees weak. Arms were heavy. There was vomit on my sweater already, grandma's spaghetti, I was nervous! I came within three feet of him, reaching out my arm to pet him, and hoping he might pet me back. But then... SLAP!! A riveting sound echoed against the rocks. Water sprayed in the air! What looked like a waffle levitated above the water, mere inches from my face, and then slammed the water. I was puzzled! We were miles from the nearest IHOP. What could this be? A creature emerged from under the water, the same creature that just moments earlier I had mistaken for a wild otter. This was no otter! This was a miniature beast with a tale shaped like breakfast. She whipped her face around, revealing the cold gaze of eyes that have seen battle. As she stared into my frightened soul, I noticed two of the most ginormous barf-yellow tinted buck teeth I had ever seen. It didn't take long for me to realize... this was a beaver, and she was angry... at me! I turned and bolted for my grandparents, unsure of what help they could provide. Perhaps the meatballs could be weaponized. She, in turn, began her pursuit. I soon found myself chased by a beaver, my toes inches from the strongest jaws and sharpest teeth I'd ever encountered. The shore was not too far off, and within seconds my feet touched ground, and I ran for my life! Oh, my poor grandparents, I wondered how scared they must have been to see me in such turmoil. I approached my grandma, ready to comfort her from the heart attack I had nearly given her. As I approached her, she was on the ground with my grandad... laughing hysterically!

I've survived seagulls, puppies, beavers... oh my. And so many more. In the words of Beyoncé "I'm a survivor." And in the words of Jay-Z "I've got 99 problems" - and most of them have four legs and teeth.

I've been a survivor since birth. Born blue and unable to breath, the doctors placed my life-less body in the hands of my father for one final hug. That wouldn't be the last time he held my dying body in a hospital. The second time was not that long ago actually, when stage four cancer wreaked havoc on my frail body and my wife Alyson was told to make funeral plans.

Yes, I have survived many things in my life, but cancer was not one of them. And no this is not being published posthumously, I'm still here. I just truly feel I did not survive cancer. I don't believe anyone survives cancer. To every person out there who has had to fight cancer in any of its ugly forms, you are not a survivor. You didn't *survive* cancer, you BEAT cancer. You are not a cancer survivor, you are a cancer conqueror. You are undefeated! Not everyone beats cancer. I've lost plenty a friend and family member to cancer, including my own grandma. But to those of us who are lucky enough to walk away from the fight, we walk away as champions. We don't always walk away. Sometimes we limp away. Sometimes our walking is replaced by a wheelchair or cane. We bear the scars of warriors who have taken a beating. We awake from nightmares of memories that haunt us. We lose hair from the chemicals that both saved us and weakened us. In all our suffering and loss, it is easy to view ourselves as victims. But we are victors. Cancer robbed us, but it didn't ruin us. There were many battles but only one war, and we won. That makes the score 1-0. That makes us undefeated, victorious, champions. I am not a cancer survivor, I am a cancer conqueror. This mindset makes all the difference.

I'm betting that you have been through a lot. You have battled and fought. From birth, as soon as life gave to you, it simultaneously took a lot from you. Sometimes it has felt like life took more than it gave. You've considered giving up.

You've been beaten to the core, weakened and tired from the fight, you've even self-medicated in ways that were more harmful than helpful. But you know what? You're still breathing. You're reading this book and that means you're still here. You're alive. You haven't given up. Why? Because you're not a victim, you're a victor. You're not a chump, you're a champion. The score is 1-0, and you are undefeated. There's only one way you lose and that's when you give up!

I learned this truth on a dark and dismal night, as I scanned my hospital room for something sharp, something fatal.

When, in a moment of heartbreak and despair, my trembling fingers slowly typed into Google "easy ways to die."

PART TWO:
Easy Ways To Die

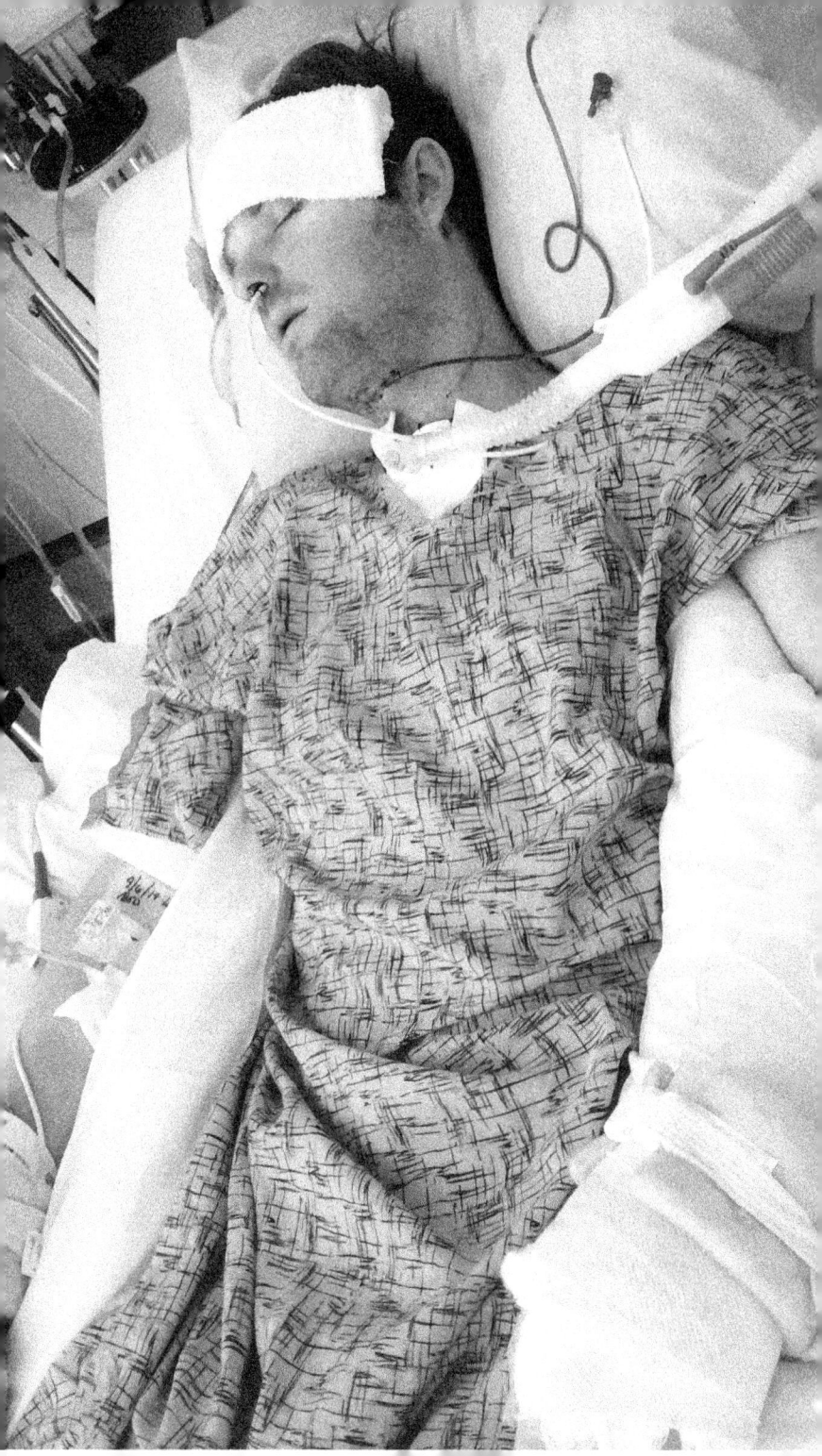

I wanted to kill myself.

Quickly. And with as little pain as possible.

The phrase "easy ways to die" stared back at me from my iPhone screen. I couldn't find the strength to press the Google Search button, too scared of the results that might pop up. I found out later that Google suggests calling 1-800-273-8255, the National Suicide Prevention Lifeline. But I didn't follow through that night. Instead, I planned out my own easy way to die. It involved a bridge and a lot of water. I later told my wife "at least the view will be beautiful as I'm falling."

Just six months previous, in March of 2016, I had been diagnosed with tongue and throat cancer. I had never smoked. Never chewed. Never drank alcohol. Never abused drugs. Growing up in a conservative Christian home, there were a lot of things I hadn't done. And yet, here I was suffering from a cancer typically caused by years of chewing tobacco. The doctors couldn't explain it. "Extremely bad luck" is how one doctor put it.

Shortly after being diagnosed my body locked up, lost all heat and I had a seizure that left me lying on the bathroom floor screaming in pain. My wife called the paramedics, the ambulance came, and thirteen days later I was released from the hospital having endured several biopsies, body scans, and a hip surgery that left me in a wheelchair for the foreseeable future. The consensus? The cancer was spreading, having just crossed the line from stage three to stage four, and an aggressive surgery was imminent.

They removed 20% of my tongue, half the lymph nodes in my neck, and placed 35 staples on my hip. Three weeks later the skin on my leg had started to grow over the staples, and one by one the staples had to be ripped out of my leg. They had not anticipated this scenario, and had nothing to give me that would numb the pain. It was a rough couple months.

May 2016
I began recovering from all the operations and surgeries. It was over. The cancer was gone.

June 2016
My tongue began to swell up. The pain began to increase until I could hardly speak or eat anymore. Another biopsy. Another scan. Another diagnosis.

July 2016
I got the phone call. The cancer had returned with a vengeance and was spreading faster than before. They were concerned that if they didn't operate soon, the cancer would kill me. I was terrified. And yet, at the same time, I felt numb.

August 2016
I met with the entire medical team, and as they began to describe in graphic detail what the next journey of my life would look like, it was more than my wife and I could bear. She collapsed to the ground, blacking out. I sat there in silence and tears as the voices of the doctors faded into the background sounding more like muffled waves washing over me, consuming me, drowning me. Have you ever been underwater in the ocean and heard the sound of waves crashing above you? That's what their voices sounded like. That's what my life felt like. I was dying.

September 2016
I underwent a fifteen hour surgery, removing an additional 60% of my tongue, and all the

lymph nodes in my neck. When I woke up in the ICU, I panicked. My body was tied down to a hospital bed. There were tubes down my neck, up my nose, and in my arms and legs. The red blinking lights and constant hums and beeps of the machines made the dark room feel even colder. They used skin and veins from my left arm to construct a new tongue, and now it was swollen three times the size of a regular tongue and I couldn't breath. To get nutrients, they placed a feeding tube through my nose but it was scratching the back of my throat, constantly eliciting a gag response. Every few minutes I felt like throwing up. The feeding tube caused a nose bleed, and as my last remaining air passage filled with blood, I began to suffocate. Having anticipated that breathing could be challenging for me, they had placed a trach through my neck and down my throat.

My body was rejecting the trach by constantly creating mucus that blocked the air hole in my neck. This meant that every five to ten minutes I could not breathe through my mouth because of my new, now swollen, tongue; I could not breath through my nose because of the blood; I could not breath through my neck because of the mucus. My heart would begin beating at an alarming rate, which would trigger the machines, which would alert the nurse who would run in with a small vacuum that would be gently shoved down my throat to vacuum the mucus so I could breath again… at least for another five to ten minutes. And this was repeated hour after hour, and after three days, I had not slept and the pain had only increased.

To help with the pain they increased my pain medication. However, pain medication can block you up from using the bathroom, so they gave me medicine that would help my body effectively get rid of waste. But on this night, after no sleep, and the constant battle to breath, I was pushed to my breaking point when one nurse ended her shift by giving me the "bathroom" medicine and the next nurse began her shift by giving me the "bathroom" medicine. All I can remember is this moment: sitting on the hospital bathroom floor, sitting in my own crap. Blood coming down my nose. Mucus pouring out my throat. And me gagging and screaming in pain as my body tried and tried to throw up but couldn't. In that moment, the most painful and dehumanizing moment of my entire life, all I could hear was the voice of one of my doctors who had warned me: "Jason, it will only get worse for the next five days, and then you'll begin to recover." But my mind was only playing back the phrase "…it will get worse for the next five days…"

Five days? I couldn't even take another five

minutes of this!

I couldn't think straight, I could hardly breath, and all I longed for was sleep and for the pain to cease. But I couldn't sleep and the pain was getting worse. And then it hit me. There was only one way to make it stop.

Death.

I wanted to die. I needed to die. I was going to kill myself. As I looked around that hospital room one more time, my trembling fingers having just typed "easy ways to die" - I tried to find something sharp, something fatal, something that could end this misery.

Have you ever been there?

Have you ever been pushed to the breaking point, exhausted from the fight, feeling you and everyone around you would be better off if you were dead?

Have you ever been so tired mentally and emotionally that you wanted to quit?

And have you ever shared those feelings with anyone?

We typically keep these types of feelings to

ourselves. We even feel ashamed of them. It's a cruel cycle. We experience painful emotions, which elicit raw feelings of anger, depression, and sometimes suicidal thoughts; and then we feel shame for having those thoughts. The shame we feel makes us more angry and depressed and suicidal… which elicits more shame. And as we bottle up the anger, depression, and shame, we begin dying on the inside. But on the outside, no one has any idea.

Whatever you feel, it is nothing to be ashamed of. There is a reason you feel the way you feel, and hurt the way you do. Your emotions are valid, and even helpful. Emotion is not the enemy. Emotions are like fire alarms. Don't ignore them. I would know.

I'm a terrible cook. I start fires.

One day I was trying to cook potato wedges for my wife. I put the wedges on a flat pan, and placed it in the oven. Then I walked away. The house began to fill with smoke but I didn't even notice because I was in the other room. The fire alarms never went off because I hated the sound they made every time I cooked. (For whatever reason, my cooking seemed to trigger the fire alarms quite often). The sound they made annoyed me, so months earlier I had removed their batteries.

My wife called 911 as the smoke began to build in the house. The fire department came, put out the grease fire, and then asked me a very important question:

"Where are your fire alarms and why are they not working?"

I tried to explain to them that fire alarms are annoying. They were not convinced.

Our emotions are like fire alarms and they are necessary. The fire alarm is not the problem, it is simply alerting you to the fact that there is a problem. Your emotions are not the problem. They are alerting you to the fact that something inside you is burning and needs to be addressed. When you turn off your fire alarms, the fire grows. When you silence and ignore your feelings, and keep them bottled up inside, you burn out.

When you are hiding, you are not healing.

The night I tried to kill myself, I was isolated and alone. I had dark thoughts and dark feelings. Even worse, I had dark beliefs. I believed I was nothing but a victim. I believed my best days were behind me. I believed the worst was yet to come. When a person has such negative thoughts and beliefs, and they find themselves isolated and alone, toxic behavior can ensue.

The doctors can't fix what you keep hidden.

What all struggles have in common is the battle that takes place in the mind and the heart. Whether it's cancer, relationship conflict, extreme debt… it can never be fixed if it remains in the dark. The battle inside must come outside. What's hiding in the shadows must be brought into the light.

I was feeling a pain like I had never felt. I was ready to kill myself. That's when my wife walked into the room.

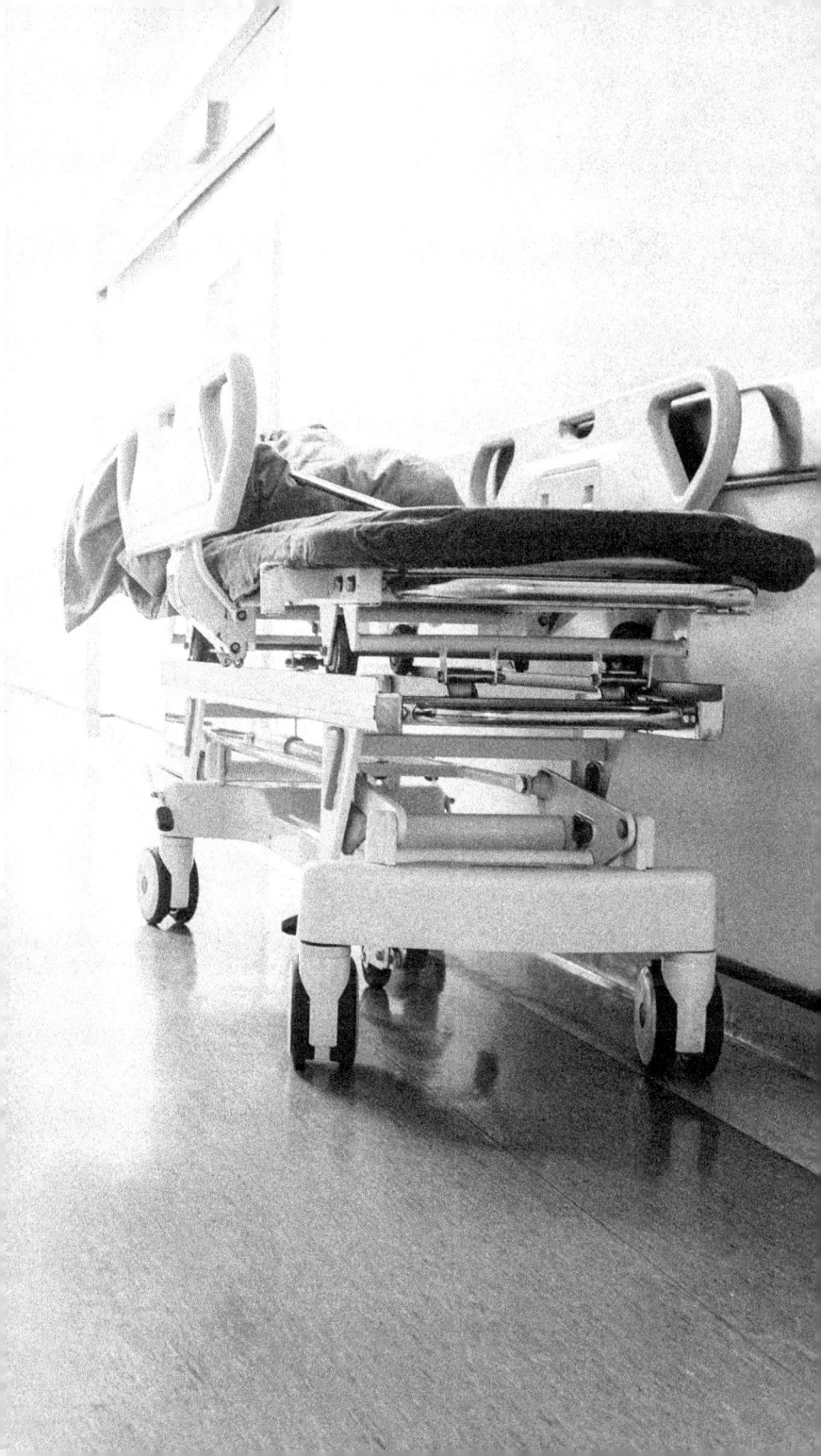

PART THREE:
Heroes & Villains

"What is a hero to you?" Mr. Brown asks.

"A hero kills people, people that wish him harm. A hero is part-human and part-supernatural. A hero is born out of a childhood trauma, or out of a disaster that must be avenged."

"OK, you're thinking of a superhero" Mr. Brown replies.

Dwight Schrute responds "We all have a hero in our heart."

- The Office

Every great story has a hero.

And every great story has a villain.

What makes a hero a hero, and a villain a villain, usually comes down to how the character responds to tragedy.

23

There can be a lot of confusion as to what makes someone a hero. All the firefighters who showed up to the collapsing Twin Towers on September 11th, 2001... some rescued people by carrying them out of the smoke and debris... some committed themselves to search and rescue, but never found anyone... some were assigned to hosing down the burning ruins... do we only count some of them as heroes? Does it only count if the hero actually rescued someone? Or are they heroes because they simply showed up when most others would have run?

I believe it's that simple.

A hero shows up.

I was on the brink of suicide and my wife showed up.

I was broken. I was hopeless. I wanted to quit.

She showed up.

Hopelessness stems from the belief that life won't get any better. The belief system that we are stuck in this moment and can't get out. Anyone who has fought a deadly disease understands this feeling. In the moment of battle, that moment feels like infinity. You can't see the future. You can't see the other side. You feel like this moment is and will be forever. You feel stuck. You feel hopeless.

Debt elicits this feeling. Divorce elicits this feeling. A car accident elicits this feeling. College loans, family conflict, middle school and high school, being single, getting sick, watching a loved one get sick… these moments feel like infinity. We feel stuck, as if life will never get better and this trauma will never end. But these are just moments.

Life is a collection of moments and the beauty about life is that no moment lasts forever. We tend to see this as a bad thing, but it's a huge blessing. Whatever pain you are fighting right now, it will not last forever. But in a dark and despairing moment, I lost sight of that truth.

Then my wife showed up.

She looked into my eyes and saw the despair. She could sense that I was far from OK, beyond the physical pain was something much worse. I was in a very dark place.

And she saved my life.

She is my hero because she didn't lecture me. She didn't quote scripture at me. She didn't tell me to feel or not feel a certain way. She simply showed up. She sat with me. She cried with me. And then she sang.

And my wife is not a singer.

But in this moment, when words could never be enough, she sang.

She was working two jobs at the time to help pay for the medical bills. Waking up at 4am to get to one job, and returning home by 9pm from the second job. She would then head to the hospital to be with me till midnight, and do it all over again the next day. That's a hero. Someone who shows up when it is inconvenient to do so. Someone who shows up with no agenda but to love and listen. Someone who showed up simply so that I wouldn't give up.

Her tired feet began to pace the room as I sat in that hospital bed contemplating suicide. Her voice, tired from a long day and an emotional season, began to sing. The flashing lights and constant beeping of the machines began to drown into background noise as the sound of her voice echoed through the halls. She didn't get the lyrics right. She didn't hit all the right notes. But in my darkest moment, her voice was as beautiful as any singing voice I have ever heard. She sang for an hour, pacing that room, tears slowly cascading from her face and hitting the dark cold hospital floor. I felt something truly beautiful that night. It was as if Peace was a presence that entered the room and whispered me to sleep. My eyes grew heavy. My thoughts calmed down. And for the first time in three days, I drifted off to sleep.

She saved my life. She is my hero.

Every great story has a hero. Every great story also has a villain.

There is very little that separates a hero from a villain. Initially. The origin story of any hero and any villain is quite similar. Tragedy is at the heart of both stories. The hero is simply the one who chose to get better, not to get bitter. The villain is the one who takes the pain, hate, and anger of their experience and turns it on others or even themselves. Both have similar origins, but how they respond to tragedy determines if they are labeled hero or villain in the story. Both are victims of life's unexpected disappointments. Spider-Man was an orphan. Iron Man was a prisoner. Star-Lord's mom died of cancer. Any one of these heroes were given the recipe to become great villains. But when you stop viewing yourself as the victim, when you get your eyes off of your own pain and look around to see the pain and suffering of everyone around you, and when you reject bitterness, unforgiveness, and despair, you change the narrative of your own story. You become the hero.

But we love to be the victims. We love feeling sorry for ourselves. We love the attention it brings. We love feeling justified in our anger and resentment toward people who hurt us. We often don't want to heal because then we could no longer be the victim. Victims get to blame others for the consequences of their own decisions. Victims get to stay angry and still receive people's sympathy. And as the bitterness and darkness grows inside… victims become villains.

How will you respond to the tragedy in your life? Will you be the hero or the victim?

Take a look at this cloud below. What do you think of when you see this grey cloud?

Typically, when adults see clouds in the sky, they think to themselves "the weather could be better." Or perhaps they think "a storm is coming." Or perhaps they think nothing of it.

But a child can look at that same cloud and yell "I see a bunny!" Or "Do you see the dragon? There's his eyes, and there's the fire coming out of his mouth!" A kid will see the same grey cloud and her imagination will come to life. She will piece together an entire story from that one grey cloud. She will see animals in the sky, and mythological creatures like unicorns. She will laugh at the same cloud that sparked fear and disappointment in the mind of an adult. We know better, as adults, right? We know what that cloud really represents. It represents less sun. It represents colder weather. But to a child, that cloud is a character in a story that brings joy and inspiration. If only we could look at the world the way a child does.

How you and I view our world, and view ourselves in this world, influences the trajectory of our story. Our belief system can either help us or hurt us. Our response to tragedy will be our legacy. The tragedy itself is not our legacy, our pain does not define us. What we do with the pain defines us.

I refuse to be the "cancer" guy because I will not be defined by my tragedy. I will be remembered for how I overcame my tragedy. You have the same opportunity. How will you handle your pain?

Many of us hide our pain and then attempt to numb it. Instead of getting professional help, we get help from a bar or liquor store... or worse. We drink to numb the pain. We self-medicate to numb the pain. We eat to numb the pain. We cut ourselves to numb the emotional pain because physical pain hurts less than what we are feeling inside, and what's happening on the outside can distract us from the real problem and the real fire that is burning within. When we go down this unhealthy road, we become the very people we swore we'd never be. We become like our drunken father. We become like our abusive uncle. We become the villain in someone else's story.

It doesn't have to be this way. Tragedy does not have to define us. Cancer is not the main character in my story, and I refuse to be upstaged by it. It is merely the tragedy that set in motion the events for me to either become the hero or the villain.

The morning after my wife ṣang over me and saved me from myself, I chose life. I chose not to give up. I chose not to get bitter. They told me I'd never sing or speak again. I was determined to prove them wrong. They told me I might never walk again. I was determined to run.

Eight weeks of chemotherapy. Thirty five rounds of radiation. Nine months of no talking, no eating, no singing. I lost 80 pounds. I lost my ability to speak. I lost my ability to taste. I lost feeling in my left arm. I lost my ability to play piano. I lost music. I lost pleasure. I lost family time. I lost date nights. I lost so much... but I was determined to gain as much of it back as possible.

I spent months in speech therapy, working relentlessly to get my speech back. I spent hours upon hours warming up my vocals, just trying to sing one simple lyric. And I spent days at the piano, writing music with one arm.

July 2nd, 2017
To celebrate my road to recovery and thank those who had supported me in my journey, after months or relearning how to speak and how to sing again, I walked on stage to sing an original song I had written called "These Walls."

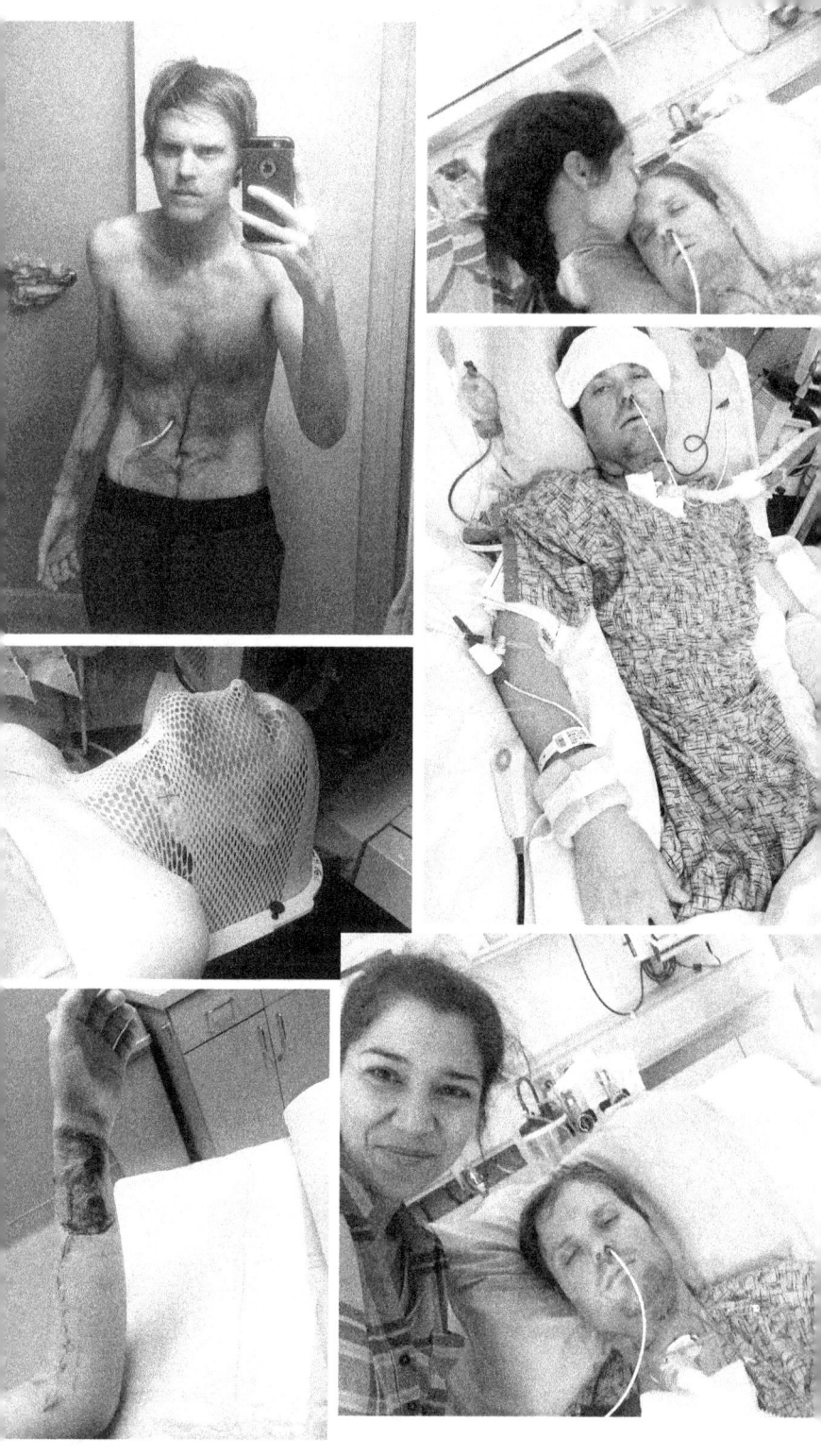

PART FOUR:
These Walls

"You are greater than these walls I'm circling.

You are stronger than this army that I see.

You are bigger than the mountains that I face,

And I will choose to only praise You.

This is my song. This is my dare.

To worship You, even as these walls are standing there."

I should be dead right now.

At one point my wife was told to "prepare for his funeral." I'm incredibly grateful to the talented doctors at UCSD who removed the cancer and recreated a tongue. I'm beyond thankful to my wife who saved my life the night I was ready to kill myself. I'm appreciative to every one of my friends and family who offered prayers and support. It's a miracle I'm even alive to write this book. But the greater miracle was the day I sang my song "These Walls" to a packed auditorium of friends and a congregation who had supported me in so many ways through my journey and fight with cancer.

I didn't get all the lyrics right. I didn't hit all the right notes. But I sang. For the first time ever, I sang a song I had written, with a tongue that couldn't move. To this day, I can hardly move my tongue, but I'm still singing. It's easy to sing when life is going perfect. The challenge is to sing when the walls are standing before you. To sing when you feel like weeping. To sing when the only desire you have is to give up. To sing when you don't even have the words to speak. I sang my song with all the energy I could muster. I went home exhausted and slightly embarrassed. My voice had cracked, my speech impediment was extremely noticeable, and my new lisp made me feel insecure and unsure if people could even understand me.

Then the unexpected happen.

My song was uploaded to Facebook around midnight the following Thursday. Marketing strategists will tell you what a horrible idea it is to post a video at midnight on a Thursday! No one should have seen it, save for a faithful few who followed on Facebook. But somehow, within two days, the video of me singing "These Walls" had attracted over 100,000 views and hundreds of comments from people all over the country. A week later it crossed one million views, and thousands upon thousands of comments. The phones wouldn't stop ringing, and I couldn't check my emails fast enough.

Within two weeks the song had been translated into over 20 different languages and was being sung every Sunday by churches in Australia, Canada, China, France, Germany, India, Japan, Mexico, New Zealand, Norway, The Philippines, Singapore, Spain, Sweden, Russia and quite a few more that I lost track of! Over six million people had seen the video, and now my wife and I were getting calls from CBN, FOX, NBC and the 700 Club, wanting to interview us and share our story around the globe.

Within one year, I had gone from contemplating suicide while laying in my own filth on a cold hospital bathroom floor... to this. To be honest, it was too overwhelming. Every day I was having conversations with people all over the country, and these were emotional conversations. I spoke with people who had less than two weeks to live. I spoke with people who had just lost a loved one to cancer. I spoke with people who had the same type of tongue cancer and were scared beyond belief. My inbox had hundreds and hundreds of unread emails, and I eventually replied to each one of them, but it took months.

In all the craziness that followed, there were a few phone calls and emails I will never forget. In fact, I took some of the following stories, and featured them in the official music video for "These Walls."

One lady had a condition that was causing uncontrollable nerve pain in her hands. She had been a painter for years, but after the condition began getting worse, she quit. Then she saw the video "These Walls" and picked up her paintbrush and began to paint again. She even sent me photos of her new paintings.

One man had been a piano player and worship leader but was shot. After seeing "These Walls" he decided to move past the pain and return to the piano.

One girl had been a singer, and just like me, her tongue had been removed due to cancer. She hated the new sound of her voice and quit singing. Then she saw "These Walls" and began to sing again. She even sang my song "These Walls" to a packed house, and sent me the video. It moved me to tears. She later flew to San Diego to meet me.

Story after story, I began to meet and hear from incredible people who had overcome tragedy or were battling tragedy, who were refusing to give up or get bitter. Society would call them victims, but they were proving society wrong. These weren't victims... these were victors, champions, and heroes.

I remember sitting in the hospital, receiving chemotherapy, surrounded by dozens of other patients hooked up to their chemo machines, fighting cancer. Some were bald. Some were balding. Many, like me, were extremely skinny and appeared weak. To the rest of the world, this looked like a room full of sick people. Weak people. Victims. But I know the truth. It takes the heart of a champion to fight cancer. It takes the heart of a champion to support a loved one fighting cancer. It takes strength to wake up every day in a hospital and not give up. Hospitals aren't full of weak sick people... they are full of some of the strongest warriors this world has even been privileged to know.

You are stronger than you know. You have more potential than you are even aware of. Your past is only half the story, the finale is in the future.

You have the potential to be heroic, not just in your story, but in someone else's.

I kept it a secret for months that I was battling cancer. Almost no one knew. But one day, my friend posted a Go Fund Me link on Facebook for my wife and I to help pay for the medical bills. All of a sudden my Facebook page blew up! Within a couple hours over 200 Facebook friends had commented on my timeline, saying the nicest things I have ever read:

"Jason's music inspired me and changed my life."

"I grew up listening to Jason's music, and it helped me get through high school."

"Jason was so inspiring and kind to me."

"Jason was a good friend."

"Jason was so talented."

"Jason was…"

Jason was.

I felt like I had attended my own funeral. It's a rare blessing to get to see what people really think about you when they think you are dying. I didn't know half these people even cared about my existence. Some of them were old friends that I hadn't spoken to in years. Some were people I had a falling out with. Some were extremely talented artists that I looked up to. I never knew these people felt so much love toward me, and it got me thinking.

Why do we wait until people are dead or dying to say these things?

We constantly withhold compliments. We are quick to criticize but slow to praise. We wait until it is too late to tell someone they are loved. When someone impresses us, we keep silent. When someone disappoints us, we raise our voice. How is that heroic?

I realized in that moment that I do the same thing. There are so many people that have blessed me. So many people that I am inspired by. So many people that I have the kindest thoughts toward. Yet rarely have I ever told them. Why not? I have no good reason not to tell them. The truth is, life is challenging, we need all the encouragement we can get. We can be heroes by simply telling people the good things we feel toward them... before they are on their deathbed.

I wish I had known earlier how these friends felt about me. It would have encouraged me sooner in my dark times. I am determined to do the same for others. It's life-giving. Words of encouragement are like speaking life into someone. And when tragedy strikes in their life, your words just might be the extra strength they need to keep fighting. You could be the hero for someone else, as my wife was for me. She spoke life when all I could think about was death.

Speak life. Not just in the life of someone else, but in your own life as well. Speak life into your situation, speak hope into your storm. And when you don't have the words to speak… sing. Sing when you feel you've hit a wall. When the armies surround you and the mountain prevents you from moving further, sing. Until the walls come crumbling down, lift your head up and sing. Tragedy will not have the final say in your story.

How we respond to tragedy says everything about us.

We can focus on what we've lost, or we can focus on beating the odds. We can view ourselves as victims and give up, feeling completely justified in doing so, or we can press on and inspire others to do the same. We never know who is watching, but your decision to not give up on yourself just might save someone else's life. I've talked with many who had been in my shoes, wanting to kill themselves, but as they watched me choose life, my decision in turn saved theirs.

That's the power we have. We can save lives simply but not giving up on ours.

So lift up your head, wipe the tears from your eyes, and dream again. What have you given up on in the battle? What have you quit doing because of the fight?

Were you an artist? Paint again.

Were you a dancer? Dance again.

Were you a musician? Play again.

Were you a singer? Sing again.

Were you in love? Love again.

Were you optimistic? Hope again.

Don't let tragedy rob you of anything more than it already has. I didn't give up, and now millions across the world are singing my song.

I didn't ask to be anyone's hero.

But I refused to be the victim.

Printed in the USA
CPSIA information can be obtained
at www.ICGtesting.com
JSHW061236060324
58472JS00015B/175

9 781734 690408